New Action Sports

Mastering Martial Arts

by Steve Potts

CAPSTONE PRESS

MANKATO

Capstone Books are published by Capstone Press
151 Good Counsel Drive, P.O. Box 669, Mankato, Minnesota 56002
http://www.capstone-press.com

Library of Congress Cataloging-in-Publication Data
Potts, Steve, 1956-
    Mastering martial arts/Steve Potts
    p. cm.
    Includes bibliographical references and index.
    Summary: Discusses the history, techniques, and training related to karate,
judo, and kung fu.
    ISBN 1-56065-404-X
    1. Martial atrs--Training--Juvenile literature. [1. Martial arts.] I. Title.
GV1102.7 T7P69 1996
796.8--dc20   95-52010
                                                                   CIP
                                                                    AC

Photo Credits
Archive Photos, 28, 30, 38
Archive Photos/Fox, 19
Archive Photos/London Daily Express, 39
Peter Ford, cover, 11, 14, 17, 40, 43
Unicorn Stock Photos,4
Unicorn Stock Photos/Dick Young, 8
Unicorn Stock Photos/Ed Harp, 12, 26
Unicorn Stock Photos/Florent Flipper, 6, 22
Unicorn Stock Photos/Joseph Fontenot, 36
Unicorn Stock Photos/Russell Grundke, 25
Unicorn Stock Photos/Sue Vanderbilt, 20, 33, 34, 42

2 3 4 5 6 05 04 03 02 01

Table of Contents

Words in **boldface** type in the text are defined
in the Glossary in the back of this book.

Chapter 1
The Martial Arts

It takes many hours of long, hard practice to become good at the martial arts. Students of karate, judo, and kung fu must master many exercises and **techniques** to become experts in their sport.

Karate

Most North American students learn a form of karate that comes from Okinawa. This is an island southwest of Japan. It was settled more than 1,000 years ago by people from China. Many movies show karate masters using this martial art.

Martial arts students work hard to become experts.

Judo

Judo is another popular martial art. Many students begin judo lessons to learn to defend themselves. The lessons become an introduction to the tough training that judo requires. Judo trains both the mind and the body.

Kung Fu

Movies have made kung fu one of the most popular martial arts. Kung fu came to North America from China in 1958. That was when Bruce Lee moved to the United States.

Lee was from Hong Kong. He had studied kung fu in China. In the United States, he had a part-time job washing dishes to help pay for college. Some of his fellow students learned that Lee had studied kung fu. Lee quit washing dishes to teach kung fu classes.

Lee became famous as a kung fu master and movie actor. Thousands of people learned about kung fu by watching Bruce Lee in the movies.

Children of all ages take martial arts classes.

Chapter 2
Karate

Karate classes give students skills in self-defense. Karate also teaches students how to use their willpower. It allows them to accomplish goals they did not think were possible.

Karate is popular with athletes from other sports. Skaters and basketball players find that karate helps them condition their bodies. Karate also conditions the mind. Many athletes feel that karate training gives them an extra edge that keeps them competitive.

Karate conditions the mind as well as the body.

Advanced Training

Beginning karate students become familiar with the **dojo.** They master the basic techniques of karate. Then they learn many new exercises when they begin advanced karate training.

Advanced karate classes move much faster than beginning classes. Students learn katas. A kata is series of movements in an arranged order. The hands and feet move in many different positions during a kata.

Students practice katas for many hours. They can practice with partners or by themselves. Karate requires that katas be practiced again and again.

As they do katas, students learn to control their breathing. Katas strengthen their muscles. They develop coordination. The perfect kata starts and finishes in the same position. Though katas look easy, it takes many years of practice to do them the right way.

Students learn katas in advanced karate classes.

Other Exercises

Advanced karate students do an exercise called free fighting. Two students fight against each other. Students come onto the mat. They bow to each other. Then they begin to fight.

They may try any move they would use against a real opponent. All their hours of practice are put to the test. To succeed, fighters need to think and move quickly.

Advanced students also work with the makiwara, which is a board about four feet (1.2 meters) high. The center of the board is padded with sponge or rubber. It is covered with canvas. Students try to punch or kick the padded center. Students often try to hit the same small area 40 or 50 times during one practice. This improves the control of their punches and kicks.

Some karate students use the iron geta. This is a sandal made of iron that weighs about five pounds (2.25 kilograms). Students wear the sandals during practice to help make their legs and ankles stronger.

Karate teaches concentration and discipline.

Chapter 3
Judo

Jigoro Kano made modern judo popular in the 1880s. It spread from Japan throughout the world. Kano gave demonstrations in North America to two United States presidents, Ulysses S. Grant and Theodore Roosevelt. Roosevelt and his son learned judo in the White House. Roosevelt often surprised visitors by trying out his judo skills on them.

Judo is a good way for people to defend themselves. In 1914, it was popular among some women in England. They were protesting to win the right to vote.

When it is done right, a judo fall is painless.

People attacked the women during their protests. So they studied judo for self-defense. Some of the women created the Bodyguard. This was a secret group that sometimes fought the police so other women could give speeches.

Today, judo is popular in Japan, Europe, and North America. There are thousands of people who study basic and advanced judo skills.

Advanced Training

Judo students must first learn to fall safely. After that, they learn several other important exercises.

The standing throw teaches students how to throw and how to fall. One partner stands still and does not fight. The other partner tries to throw the opponent to the mat. After trying this five or 10 times, the partners switch to learn the other technique.

Groundwork exercises teach students the best ways to escape during practice and competition.

A judoist keeps a good grip on an opponent during a throw.

Groundwork is practiced on the mat. Students let other students put them in a hold or a lock. Then they try to break out. If they are successful, they escape. If they cannot escape, they admit defeat.

Randori is an exercise that allows students to practice freely. First they bow to each other. Then they try moves on each other. Partners attack, defend, and throw each other.

Randori is a way to test what students have learned. It is not a competition. Students try to help each other. They do not try to see who is the best.

Advanced judo students sometimes participate in katas. Kata demonstrations are like classes. Katas are designed to show how judo moves should be taught and learned.

Exercises

Judo students learn exercises that strengthen their bodies. They do push-ups on their palms or on their closed fists. This makes their arms stronger.

Young women took judo lessons in the 1950s. The martial arts are attractive to young and old.

They strengthen their fingers by holding their arms in front of their chests at shoulder level. They spread their fingers out and push one hand's fingers against the other hand's fingers. They count to five and then separate their fingers. They repeat the exercise several times.

They strengthen their wrists with a newspaper. They grab the newspaper in one corner with one hand. They hold it in front of their body at shoulder height. While the newspaper is hanging, they use the hand holding the paper to wrap it into a ball. They repeat this exercise with the other hand.

Judo students make their legs stronger by crouching down. They put their hands on their knees and walk around the mat in a crouched position.

Games

Judo students learn games that test their skills. One game is called One in the Middle. One student is blindfolded and seated in the center of a mat. The other students gather at the edge of the mat.

Martial arts classes are often available after school.

They try to sneak past the blindfolded student. If the blindfolded student can catch another student and place him or her in a judo hold, the blindfold comes off. The captured student takes the place in the center of the mat.

Another game is called Diving. One student crouches on the mat. Other students dive over the student on the mat. They roll out of their dives like they would during a fall.

Anyone who does not complete the fall correctly drops out of the game. After the first round, a second student crouches on the floor next to the first student. The other students attempt their dives again. Then a third student is added. The game is repeated until everyone has dropped out. Diving is a good way to practice falling skills.

Contests

Advanced judo students often sign up for judo competitions. These are called shiai. Competitors score points by throwing their

Martial arts competitions are popular.

opponents to the mat or by holding their opponents to the mat. They try to choke or lock them until they give up.

Competitions are used to grade students. They are used to check students' progress and to award belts. Students usually compete against others of the same weight with the same grade of belt. Competitions are held across North America.

Winners take home prizes and trophies. They also have the satisfaction of testing their skills in front of their teachers, friends, family, and other students. Judo competitions test whether the students' training has prepared their bodies and minds successfully.

Winners of martial arts competitions take home trophies.

Chapter 4

Kung Fu

Kung fu originated at the Shaolin Monastery in China more than 1,000 years ago. The monastery was in an isolated area of China. The **Buddhist** monks there were looking for a way to defend themselves against robbers and thieves.

As part of their religious training, the monks learned to breathe in a special way. They breathed very slowly and deeply and held their breath. This is called **ch'i** breathing. It helped the monks concentrate.

Bruce Lee was a famous kung fu master and movie star.

The monks also tried to strengthen their muscles. They learned to stretch muscles so they could meditate longer. Meditating is thinking deeply for a long time. They could meditate for several hours.

The monks also learned exercises to defend themselves. Kung fu masters today teach their students these same punches and kicks.

The monks did not believe in using violence. Modern kung fu teachers hope their students use the training only for self-defense. Teachers also hope their students learn the philosophy of kung fu along with the self-defense skills. The best kung fu student is one who can control both thoughts and actions.

Advanced Training

Kung fu students begin their formal training by learning the proper **stance.** They must know how to place their body, feet, and legs before trying any other skill.

Buddhist monks in an isolated area in China started kung fu more than 1,000 years ago.

There are 10 popular stances in kung fu. Many stances imitate animals. In the Horse Stance, students sit as they would on a horse's back. Students who look like they are about to jump up off the ground are probably trying the Cat Stance.

Each stance teaches different things. Some stances strengthen arm muscles. Other stances improve coordination. Students practice these stances for many hours. They learn how to be patient. They learn endurance. Many beginning students quit kung fu classes because they do not have the discipline to practice.

After mastering several stances, kung fu students learn how to step forward and back. They also switch from stance to stance. After many hours of practice at changing from one stance to another, kung fu students can do this without much effort.

Learning Defense
Next, students learn to use their arms, hands, feet, and legs to defend themselves. The hands and feet must move together.

Parents and children can practice the martial arts together.

The feet can also be used as weapons. Students learn which parts of the feet provide the best defense. They learn to kick with the sides, heel, and ball of the foot. That way they do not break their toes. Then students learn how to kick to the front, back, and sides without losing their balance.

The next step for the kung fu student is to learn a set. A set is a group of movements designed by the teacher. Sets are practiced many times.

The usual set is a mixture of stances, blocks, kicks, and strikes. By practicing the same moves over and over, students increase their speed and improve their concentration.

Weapons

The best kung fu students are taught how to use weapons. The Shaolin monks used swords, boat oars, and sticks. Kung fu masters teach students that a weapon is like another part of the body.

Students learn to practice the same movements with weapons as they do with their hands. They hope they will never have to use weapons. If they do, though, they will be ready to defend themselves or other people.

Some martial arts students are taught to use weapons.

Advanced students can break boards by kicking them.

The Iron Palm

After weapons training, kung fu students sometimes learn the iron palm. It is a technique that looks almost magical.

Students start by pushing their hands into a jar filled with sand. They do this exercise several times each day. After each session, they rub their hands with a medicine made from **herbs.** The medicine softens their hands.

Once the students are comfortable with the sand, they try the same exercise with pebbles and small rocks. The last thing they try is iron ball bearings. They have mastered the iron palm when they can shove their hands into a jar of iron ball bearings and not hurt their hands. Kung fu masters know they must always use medicine or their hands will be hurt.

Superpowers

Students who master the iron palm technique seem to have superpowers. They can break boards or even a stack of bricks with their bare hands. This exercise is dangerous, though. Good kung fu teachers make sure their students are well trained before they try it.

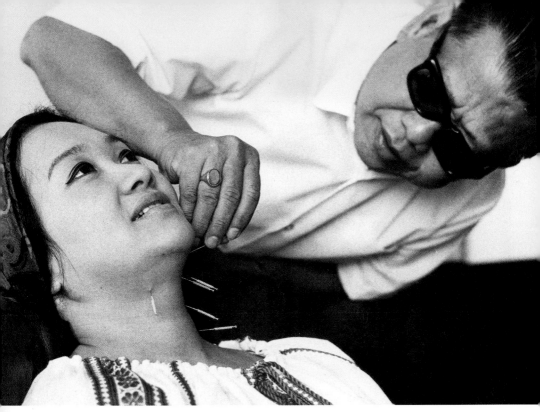
Acupuncurists put needles into the body along ch'i lines.

The Ch'i

The most advanced kung fu students learn ch'i techniques. It is hard for many North American students to understand ch'i. People can feel ch'i. But it has no color, shape, or smell.

Ch'i helps the body do what it must do to operate. The Chinese believe that ch'i runs through the human body along certain lines.

They are like highways. These lines are what Chinese healers use when they practice **acupuncture.**

Acupuncturists put needles into the body along the ch'i lines. The needles change the ch'i. This improves a person's health.

Acupuncture is an ancient Chinese art of healing that uses needles to adjust the ch'i in the body.

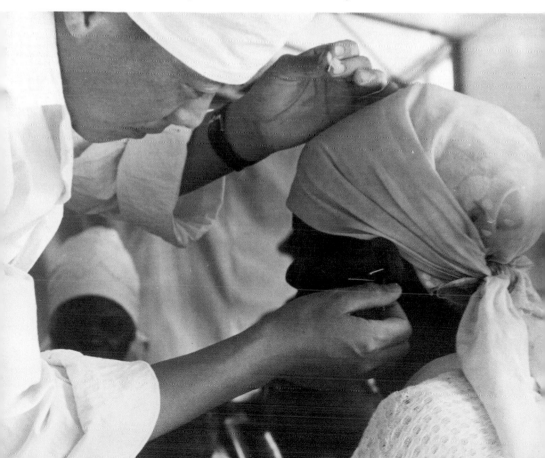

Kung fu students who practice ch'i exercises can do amazing things. They can raise heavy rocks or furniture by themselves. They seem to have magical powers.

Meditation

Kung fu masters teach their students meditation. This helps them control their ch'i. Meditation is often done in positions that look uncomfortable to someone who is not familiar with them.

Students might sit on the floor and cross their legs. They might lie down on the floor and raise their arms. They might stand for a long time with a leg or an arm raised.

If kung fu masters continue meditation for several years, they develop nai gung. This is a special inner power. It allows students to link their physical, mental, and spiritual powers and control them.

Training in the martial arts is tough.

Kung fu masters can make their bodies seem light or heavy by controlling this power. They can be hit very hard and not seem to feel any pain. They can also jump very high.

Kung Fu Medicine

The monks at Shaolin Monastery were interested in being as fit as they could be. Their exercises and training made them very healthy.

If one monk was hurt while training, another monk used medicine to treat the injury. Kung fu training is very tough. Sometimes the monks broke their arms or legs or were hit in the eye. Some were knocked out while practicing their kicking exercises.

Kung fu students learn to put special herbs on wounds and cuts. They also learn where to tap the bottom of the foot to wake up someone who is knocked out. Kung fu teaches its students to be physically strong and mentally powerful. It is one of the most popular martial arts.

It takes hours of practice to become an expert in the martial arts.

Glossary

acupuncture—the ancient Chinese art of healing that uses needles to adjust the ch'i in the body, creating good physical and mental health

Buddhist—person who practices Buddhism, an important religion and philosophy in China, Japan, Korea, and Southeast Asia

ch'i—a Chinese alphabet character that means life force or breath

dojo—the center where martial arts training takes place

herbs—plants that can be used as medicine

stance—a special way to stand

techniques—the way a person uses skills to make something artistic or to make something happen

Students of the martial arts master many exercises and techniques to become experts.

To Learn More

Gutman, Bill. *Judo*. Action Sports. Minneapolis: Capstone Press, 1995.

Gutman, Bill. *Karate*. Action Sports. Minneapolis: Capstone Press, 1995.

Gutman, Bill. *Kung Fu*. Action Sports Minneapolis: Capstone Press,1995.

Knotts, Bob. *Martial Arts*. New York: Children's Press, 2000.

Randall, Pamela. *Kung Fu*. Kids' Library of Martial Arts. New York: PowerKids Press, 1999.

Tagliaferro, Linda. *Bruce Lee*. Biography. Minneapolis: Lerner Publications, 2000.

You can read articles about martial arts in *Black Belt* and Inside *Kung Fu* magazines.

Useful Addresses

Judo Canada
266-1725 St. Laurent
Ottawa, ON K1G 3V4
Canada

University of Martial Arts and Sciences
14-3650 Longstaff Road
Suite 127
Woodbridge, ON L4L 9A8
Canada

USA Karate-do Federation
P.O. Box 77083
Seattle, WA 98177-7083

U. S. Judo Association
21 North Union Boulevard
Colorado Springs, CO 80909

Index